BITCOIN FOR BOOMERS

COPYRIGHT © 2021   MICHAEL LOUNSBURY
ALL RIGHTS RESERVED
ISBN: 979-8-4752-6822-3

DEDICATION

This book is dedicated to those who seek for knowledge
and understanding and to our
Creator God through whom all knowledge comes. "But
seek first the kingdom of God and
His righteousness and all these things shall be added unto
you."
Matt: 6:33

ACKNOWLEDGMENTS

First and foremost, I would like to thank my wife, Brooke for encouraging me to learn about and invest in the cryptocurrency market. We have worked on this book together and it would not have been completed without her help. Also, I want to thank those that have shared their knowledge and experience on the internet. I learned much from Jack Spirko at thesurvivalpodcast.com, and others that share their knowledge as written video or audio presentations

CONTENTS

CHAPTER		PAGE
1	INTRODUCTION	1
2	HISTORY OF BITCOIN	5
3	WHAT IS BITCOIN AND OTHER CURRENCIES AND HOW DO THEY WORK?	8
4	HOW IS BITCOIN DIFFERENT THAN THE DOLLAR?	13
5	WHAT ARE EXCHANGES AND HOW DO THEY WORK	16
6	HOW TO OPEN A BITCOIN ACCOUNT	20
7	WHAT IS A CRYPTOCURRENCY WALLET	23
8	CRYPTOCURRENCY DEBIT CARDS	29

9	MARKET ANALYSIS	32
10	DEFINITIONS	35
11	BLOCKCHAIN USES OUTSIDE CRYPTOCURRENCY	37
	SAMPLE LEDGER	39
	NOTES	42
	ABOUT THE AUTHOR	46

CONVERT TO USD AND USE YOUR BITCOIN IN FORM OF DEBIT CARD –ANWHERE VISA OR MASTERCARD ACCEPTED

Chapter 1

Introduction

Who am I?

If you were born between the years of 1946 to 1964, you were born during the era known as the Boomer generation. I was born in 1955, smack in the middle of this time frame, a rare time in history where optimism ran high, the depression era was behind us, World War II was over, prosperity and opportunity met almost no bounds. There had never been such a prosperous time in world history. The world was our oyster, so to speak. Many of us had bought into the "American Dream", with the large house, 2 cars, and a membership at the local country club. Our leisure time was abundant. No longer did one have to slave away in the kitchen to produce a meal. Drive through fast food, pizza delivery, frozen meals and prepackaged foods abounded. As the 60's and 70's unfolded we saw the end of the Vietnam war, feminism was forefront and the equal rights movement, led by the great Martin Luther King Jr. was in full swing. It was a time of massive social and economic revolution and change.

Economically speaking, this was the era (1971) when President Nixon took the US dollar off the gold standard. This, along with the Federal Reserve and the 1913 Jekyll Island meeting was the beginning of the end for the dollar. But I am getting ahead of myself.

We have seen the advent of computers, cellphones, smart objects, You Tube, email, and a whole dictionary of new terms. It's enough to make one's head spin. We are caught in a time where our way of life is slipping away, like the Titanic, as we sit on the deck and listen to the beautiful music from the deck as it plays. Our way of life, which we so eagerly awaited, saved, put money into our stocks, savings, 401Ks and dreamed about has been turned upside down.

I am here to help and offer you a seat on a life raft. The world is changing, everything we know or knew about money is changing. If we are to preserve our wealth and prosper, we have to face this fact and go with the changing landscape. Who says you can't teach an old dog a new trick? This is a story that is playing out over thousands of families, caught in this new world we are faced with. I am here to tell you that this old dog learned, and I want to help you learn, too.

For the past 30 plus years I had been employed in the medical field as a physician assistant. I loved the work, loved the patients, and overall felt like I was making a worthwhile contribution to humanity. I glided through my years, feeling confident that at retirement I would have a substantial nest egg to live on comfortably. My wife and I would travel to see our children, who were spread out across these United States. We would take our little camper and park it by the shore of a lake or oceanfront and enjoy the well-earned freedom I had worked so hard for.

Then 2020 hit. The virus had taken over our community, as it had played out in so many cities across the world. The town I worked in was a college town. The school essentially closed its doors and only allowed online classes for almost the entire student population. I worked the walk-in clinic, and I was seeing less and less patients as the months went by.

Until that fateful day in July 2020. I had finished my shift and was getting ready for a long weekend, out fishing with my dog. "Michael, could you please come to my office," the office manager said. I sat down and she proceeded to tell me in so many words that there weren't enough patients coming through the door and that my job had been eliminated. Just like that... I never saw it coming. Earlier in the year, during an all office meeting we were assured that the loans and other financial help from the government would be sufficient to carry us through.

I left the office that afternoon, a little dazed, but relieved. After some thought I realized this was my opportunity to do something new. But I had never really given any thought to this turn of events.

1.5 years from retirement. "Well, I thought to myself, I could do locums (as needed employment in healthcare) during the winter and enjoy carefree summers working in the garden and living the American dream". So, confidently I updated my resume and sent it out to the locums staffing agencies. I waited for weeks. Nothing. Later in the year I discovered that, unlike in years past, there was record unemployment in my field. Since so many mid-level providers worked in clinics, and many offices had switched to online visits this meant many of our jobs were eliminated. This was a bit of a blow; I had never experienced this type of unemployment. I had some nest egg, and unemployment coming in. However, this didn't match what I was making in my former employment. On top of this, we had recently purchased a piece of land in which we were planning to build our dream home once I retired.

After several weeks I was getting concerned. No calls, and with my experience and excellent employment record?

While I was waiting for that phone call offering me a job, I started looking into other ways to preserve our money. Leaving our money in a savings account or even a 401K the return wasn't keeping up with inflation.

I had heard of Bitcoin a few years back, but like so many others had written it off as a fly by night scam. The markets were going crazy, and the instability of the world prompted me to learn more about cryptocurrency and what it was. My wife found a simple online course that gave us the incentive to give it a try once we understood that blockchain technology and cryptocurrencies were here to stay.

The course helped me in the most basic way to get started, however, what I write in this book will do the same, and even more.

I want to point out first and foremost I am not a financial planner, make no promises on financial gains, and to only invest with what you feel you are comfortable losing. This book is for educational purposes only.

Chapter 2

History of Bitcoin

The domain bitcoin.org was registered August 18th, 2008.

On October 31, 2008, a link to a paper authored by Satoshi Nakamoto titled *Bitcoin: A Peer-to-Peer Electronic Cash System* was posted to a cryptography mailing list. Nakamoto implemented the bitcoin software as open-source code and released it in January 2009. Nakamoto's identity remains unknown.

On January 3,2009 the bitcoin network was created when Nakamoto mined the starting block of the chain, known as the genesis block.

The first known public Bitcoin purchase, or Bitcoin Pizza Day

An unlikely use of Bitcoin was on **May 22,2010** and is known as Bitcoin Pizza Day, marking the anniversary date where in 2010 a Florida man Laszlo Hanyecz paid for two pizzas with the cryptocurrency. He paid for two pizzas with 10,000 Bitcoin. At the time of this writing, one Bitcoin is holding at around $50,000.00. Those two pizzas would be worth about half a billion dollars nowadays.

Since that time, Bitcoin has been adopted by more and more retailers, financial institutions and even countries. For example:

Retailers

- AT&T. ...
- Burger King. ...
- KFC. ...
- Overstock. ...
- Subway. ...
- Twitch
- Pizzaforcoins.com (Domino's pizza accepts through this site)
- San Jose Earthquakes (professional soccer team)
- Dish Network
- Shopify

Check out this site: https://spendbitcoins.com/places/ for many other places that accept or help you convert Bitcoin to use at merchant's stores (Amazon, WordPress, Minecraft, VRBO, and Expedia to name a few)

Mortgage lenders

Recently United Wholesale Mortgage, the nations second largest mortgage lender announced it will be accepting Bitcoin and other forms of cryptocurrency as payment for mortgages.

Countries

On September 7, 2021, El Salvador became the first country to accept Bitcoin as legal tender. Ukraine just recently recognized Bitcoin as legal tender.

According to Coinmarketcap.com there are 246 countries that have legislation in place to eventually allow Bitcoin as legal tender, including Panama, Mexico, and the US.

On the flip side are a few countries that have explicitly banned Bitcoin such as China and Russia.

Chapter 3

What is Bitcoin and Other Cryptocurrencies and How Do They Work?

Bitcoin and other cryptocurrencies are a unit of value used to make purchases and complete transactions. Bitcoin works by verifying transactions through "proof of work" then adding the transaction to the "block chain". This is a digital currency, and like the US dollar can be used to make purchases and complete transactions. Bitcoin is divided into Satoshis (named after the founder of Bitcoin, Nakamoto Satoshi). It is the smallest unit of the Bitcoin cryptocurrency and represents one hundred millionth of a Bitcoin.

Unlike the US dollar, however, which can be printed to eternity if the government entities are so inclined, **Bitcoin code set a limit of 21 million coins to be created by a process known as mining.**

Bitcoin and other cryptocurrencies are unique in that no central bank is needed to make purchases or complete transactions. This is a peer-to-peer network, in which you deal directly with the business or person involved in the transaction. This removes geographical boundaries. As long as you hold bitcoin or other cryptocurrencies and have access to a computer, transactions with other crypto holders are decentralized. The middlemen (such as central banks) are not in the equation.

We will explain how to purchase, hold, store, and make purchases with Bitcoin in subsequent chapters. Needless to say, this is where the fun begins. But for now, we will focus on how Bitcoin is different than our US dollar.

Bitcoin is mined by solving a complex mathematical equation. This equation is fully transparent to the public. It is termed a 256-bit hash value, in which a complex series of equations completes the transaction and "mines" more Bitcoin. The computer that solves the equation first is rewarded with newly created or "mined" bitcoin, which is fractionalized to 8 decimal points. The **"blockchain"** is a method of recording transactions which cannot be altered. In essence, the blockchain is an electronic ledger that cannot be changed after a transaction is completed.

"Mining" creates or puts new bitcoin into circulation by solving a mathematical puzzle. Solving this puzzle using super computers which use large quantities of electricity to operate. The people behind these super computers are called "**miners**". Computers that complete an abbreviated copy of the blockchain are called "**nodes**". This is called "**proof of work**".

Some other cryptocurrencies are now using a method called **"proof of stake"** to verify transactions. This is done by voting on the completion of a transaction. Only those who hold and stake a certain percentage of the cryptocurrency used in the transaction are allowed to verify the transaction. The "nodes" that verify the transaction are rewarded in the currency used to complete the transaction. The "node" refers to the governing body which verifies the transaction in a "proof of stake" model. Members of the governing body are rewarded in proportion or percentage of coins they stake.

About **18.78 million Bitcoins** have been mined so far, meaning 83 percent of all the Bitcoin that will ever come into existence have already been brought into circulation. This leaves a little over 2 million Bitcoins to be mined.

In summary:

- Bitcoin is a digital currency and is "mined" to create Bitcoin on the blockchain.
- Bitcoin, and other digital currencies do not need a central bank in order to complete financial transactions. This is termed peer-to-peer transactions. There are no geographical limits.
- There is finite amount of Bitcoin. Only 21 million will ever be mined.
- Proof of work is a mathematical equation that puts another Bitcoin on the blockchain
- Proof of stake is when a governing body votes on a cryptocurrency to verify a transaction.
- Both Bitcoin and other cryptocurrencies use the term "node" In Bitcoin the term means a completed blockchain. Nodes, when referring to other forms of cryptocurrencies that use proof of stake, refers to the governing body that verifies the transaction.
- About 18.78 million Bitcoins have already been mined, meaning 83 percent of all the Bitcoin have been mined.

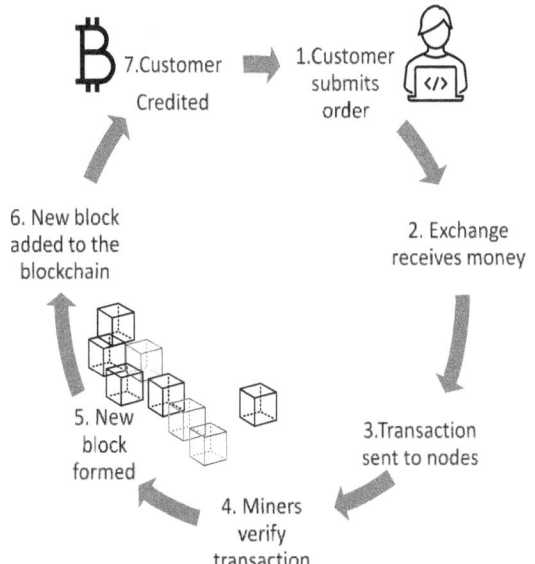

1. Customer-submits order to buy cryptocurrency from an exchange
2. Exchange receives USD from the customers bank, debit card or credit card
3. The transaction request is broadcast to a system of computers known as nodes
4. Nodes known as miners compete to verify the transaction. The node that verifies the transaction receives a payment called a "miners fee"
5. Once the transaction is verified it is added to other transactions to create a block of data
6. The new block of data is added to the blockchain where it is permanently stored and cannot be changed or altered in any way.
7. The customer is then credited with the amount of cryptocurrency they purchased minus the miner's fee and fees charged by the exchange for their service in the transaction.

Chapter 4

How Bitcoin is Different Than the Dollar

The United States dollar, the Canadian dollar, and most government issued currencies are classified as Fiat money.

Fiat money is printed or produced by a government and not backed by any commodity or asset. The government sets the value and the amount of money in circulation at any one time. There are no defined limits on the amount that can be produced. Also, the government could declare that the dollar is valueless if they so decide.

In contrast, Bitcoin is a digital currency that has a built-in code that set a limited supply. The code used to invent or produce Bitcoin set the limit at 21 million. After 21 million bitcoins have been mined or unlocked, the supply of Bitcoin will be exhausted. Also, Bitcoin is a decentralized currency which means that no government has the ability or authority to set the value of Bitcoin.

The value of Bitcoin is set by the market demand and its use as a currency for transactions. Although Bitcoin is not backed by any commodity such as silver or gold, it is backed by proof of work. This means a mathematical puzzle must be solved to mine or produce Bitcoin.

Not all cryptocurrencies have a limited supply or use proof of work for mining. One way Bitcoin is similar to the dollar is that it can be fractionalized to smaller units of value. Just like the dollar, which is fractionalized to cents. Bitcoin is fractionalized into smaller units, called

Satoshi's. One dollar is fractionalized into 100 cents, and one Bitcoin is fractionalized to 100 million Satoshi's.

FYI
You don't need to buy a whole Bitcoin

Just like 1 dollar can be fractionalized to 100 pennies, 1 Bitcoin can be fractionalized to 100,000,000 Satoshis. So you don't need to buy an entire Bitcoin. You could buy one Satoshi if you wanted to. For example, at today's rate of $46,761 for one Bitcoin:

1 Satoshi = USD $0.0004667641
So to purchase one dollars worth of Bitcoin you would be getting about 4,667 Satoshis! (Less transaction **fees, of course)**

Chapter 5

What are Exchanges and How They Work

A cryptocurrency exchange is a business that provides a marketplace where you can buy, sell, and trade cryptocurrencies. This can be done using a USD (United States dollar) currency or using other cryptocurrencies. Exchanges vary widely in the services they provide and the fees they charge for their services. Most exchanges will accept USD currency or cryptocurrency for purchases although a few exchanges will only accept cryptocurrencies. Also, you can usually store or hold your cryptocurrency on the exchange you use to make purchases.

 Some exchanges require you to transfer your purchases immediately to either a software wallet or a hardware wallet for storage. We will explain crypto wallets later, but it is a good idea to use your own personal crypto wallet for long term storage. When you purchase a cryptocurrency on an exchange there will be two types of fees involved. First there is a mining fee that goes up and down depending on the type of cryptocurrency involved and level of activity on the blockchain at the time of purchase. The mining fee will be the same on all exchanges. The second fee is charged by the exchange that facilitates the purchase of a cryptocurrency. The exchange may charge a flat fee based on the amount of the purchase. For example, they could charge a fee of $1 for any purchase under $20 and $2 for a range of $20 to

$50 and so on. Other exchanges may charge a set percentage of the transaction, such as 1% with a minimum purchase of $10 or more. Generally, the exchanges that are easier to use and provide more services will have higher fees. That being said, it may be wise to use an exchange that has higher fees but is easy to use, until you have experience in the cryptocurrency market.

Do your own research and read the explanation of fees on the exchange website before you make any purchases. Some examples of exchanges are Coinbase, Binance, Uphold, Coinex, Gemini, Kraken, Changelly and Trade Ogre.. There are many more exchanges for cryptocurrencies each with their own benefits and drawbacks. if privacy is a concern, you may want to use a non-KYC (KYC stands for "know your customer") exchange This includes identifying information such as picture ID like a passport or driver's license. The United States government requires financial institutions to collect identifying information on its customers.

Some exchanges are able to avoid this requirement by operating from a foreign country or having an online presence only. An example of a KYC exchange would be Coinbase. An example of a non-KYC exchange would be Changelly. Do your own research and use an exchange that best fits your situation. Coinbase is the first exchange I used because it is easy to navigate, but it has relatively high transaction fees.

One way to avoid high transaction or transfer fees on Coinbase is to use Coinbase Pro when sending your crypto currency to a private wallet or to another exchange. You sign in with the same password and can transfer funds between Coinbase and Coinbase Pro with no transaction fees. Once your currency is deposited into your Coinbase Pro account you can transfer it to a private wallet or another exchange for a much lower fees than using Coinbase. If you are interested in a cryptocurrency not available at one exchange you should be able to find it on another, we have accounts on several exchanges.

In addition to Coinbase, I have used Uphold which is also quite easy to navigate for a beginner in the crypto market, Uphold has lower fees but more restrictive withdrawal policies. I have also used Trade Ogre which is a non-KYC exchange. Trade Ogre does not accept USD for purchases, fees and transactions are calculated in crypto currencies. Trade Ogre requires more experience and knowledge of crypto trading to use.

That being said I found Trade Ogre to be the easiest of the non-KYC exchanges to navigate.

In summary

- Exchanges are businesses that provide a marketplace where you can buy, sell, and trade cryptocurrencies.
- Fees involved with exchanges can vary dramatically with the services they offer
- Some examples of exchanges are Coinbase, Binance, Uphold, Coinex, Gemini, Kraken, Changelly and Trade Ogre.

Chapter 6

How to Open a Bitcoin/Cryptocurrency Account

Choose an exchange that trades the cryptocurrency you are interested in. Follow instructions and prompts on the exchange to set up your account.

Some examples of established exchanges are Coinbase, Binance, Gemini, Uphold, Kraken, Trade Ogre, and many others.

Read the chapter on exchanges about the different types of exchanges and choose one that best fits your situation and level of expertise. Other options to purchase cryptocurrency, are Robin Hood, PayPal, and a few banking institutions such as Barclays and Goldman Sachs allow purchases of Bitcoin.

Do your own research and choose the option you are most comfortable with. As I had said in the previous chapter, I started with Coinbase. It is easy to learn and use.

Whichever option you choose, I believe investing in the cryptocurrency market is a wise decision and a way to increase your personal wealth. I recommend you never invest more than you can afford to lose as with all financial investments, cryptocurrency is not without risk.

By the way, please use a VPN for an additional layer of security.

In summary:

- Find an exchange that you are comfortable with. Some examples are Coinbase (where I started) Binance, Gemini, Uphold, Kraken, Trade Ogre to name a few
- You can also start buying Bitcoin (or other currencies-Litecoin, Ethereum or Bitcoin cash) on PayPal. As of this writing you may only use your cryptocurrency for PayPal purchases. There is a process for selling your cryptocurrency they outline on their site.
- Do you research, start slow and with small investments until you have some experience and understand the process.
- Use a VPN for all transactions for additional security.

Turn your dollars, which are owned and operated by central banks into decentralized currency, where you have control over your money!

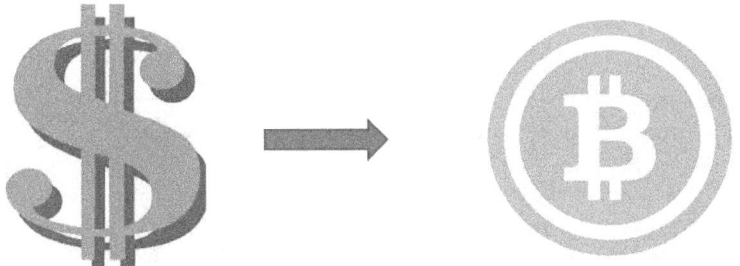

Chapter 7

What is a Cryptocurrency Wallet?

A cryptocurrency wallet is a method used to record and store information to access cryptocurrency. The advantage to this is that your cryptocurrency cannot be held up on an exchange during maintenance or periods of high trading activity. The cryptocurrency is actually always stored on the blockchain, not in the wallet. Three pieces of information are needed to access and use cryptocurrency. These are the address or location of the cryptocurrency on the blockchain, a public key and private key that are used to unlock the cryptocurrency for transfer or use.

There are three types of wallets used to store this information. The three types are a paper wallet, a software wallet and a hardware wallet.

A paper wallet is a printed page, or information written down in a notebook that contains the keys and address needed to unlock and access your cryptocurrency.

A software wallet is a program you install on your personal computer or phone which stores the information needed to access a cryptocurrency.

A hardware wallet is a device similar to a flash drive, that connects to your computer via an USB cable and contains the information needed to access your cryptocurrency.

These are all private wallets that are under your control. There are also third-party wallets which are not under your direct control, these would include wallets provided by an exchange where you purchase your cryptocurrency.

You may wish to keep some cryptocurrency on an exchange temporarily to make transfers or for temporary storage, but it is more secure to transfer your crypto assets to a private wallet for long term storage.

Examples of a software wallet are Exodus or Mycelium; these are programs you can download to your computer or mobile device to store your cryptocurrency information. These are considered hot wallets as they are connected to the Internet. They are safer and more private than a custodial wallet provided by an Exchange. But they are not as secure as a cold storage wallet.

Examples of a cold storage wallet are a paper wallet or a hardware wallet. A paper wallet has printed or written information on a piece of paper. It is considered cold storage as it is not connected to the Internet, but it can be easily damaged or destroyed. It is also labor intensive and will take up a lot of storage space when frequently updated or changed. Paper wallets are difficult to maintain and are rarely used.

A hardware wallet is a small device that resembles a flash drive or a small hard drive. Two of the most common and easiest to use hardware wallets are the Ledger and the Trezor. Each company makes two models to choose from. The most widely used and easiest to use is a Ledger nano S. I personally only use the Ledger nano S, but I believe the Trezor wallet to be an option with the same level of security. The Trezor is a little larger and so has a display that is easier to read. The device itself does not connect to the internet so it is called cold storage.

In order to transfer information into or out of the Ledger or Trezor, it must be connected to a computer or a mobile device that is capable of running the associated software or application. In order to manage and use cryptocurrency stored on a Ledger nano S you must be able to download and run the Ledger live application.

In order to use a cryptocurrency stored on the Trezor you must download and run the Trezor wallet application on your computer or mobile device. Both devices report they support over 1000 cryptocurrency coins including the most widely used cryptocurrencies such as Bitcoin and Ethereum.

If you decide to purchase a hardware wallet, purchase it from the manufacturer not from a third-party vendor such as eBay or Amazon

You can purchase the Ledger nano S at HTTPS: \\www.ledger.com

You can purchase the Trezor wallet at HTTPS: \\trezor.IO

Both the Ledger and the Trezor will require you to select an access pin. The Ledger uses a four-digit numerical pin that you select, the Trezor can be set up with a four-to-six-digit pin. Both devices will select a 24-word recovery phrase you will need to write down and store in a secure place. The recovery phase can be used to recover or restore all the information stored on your hardware wallet device. This will protect your assets from loss if your device is ever lost or damaged. The recovery phrase is randomly selected by the device. You do not select it yourself. Whoever has access to the recovery phrase can also access your assets. You never want to share your recovery phrase with anyone unless you want them to have access to your cryptocurrency assets. When you purchase a Ledger or Trezor you will receive numbered cards on which to record your phrase in the correct order, you may also want to write it down in a notebook and store it in a secure place such as a fireproof safe. After your recovery phrase is written down your device will prompt you to identify some of the words in the correct order. You will need to make correct choices before your device recovery phrase will be initiated. When you are ready to transfer your crypto assets to your device, start with a small amount for your first few transfers. That way you will avoid losing a significant amount of cryptocurrency if you make a mistake. Once you become familiar with the process, it is a good idea to transfer the majority of your cryptocurrency to a cold storage device. If you do not plan to invest in more than a few $100 in cryptocurrency, you may wish to start with a software wallet. Both Exodus and Mycelium provide a private key, which is a 12-word recovery phase instead of 24 words. They are both open-source software that is free to download and use from the Internet. Mycelium is the oldest and possibly most secure software wallet. The big drawback is Mycelium only supports Bitcoin, whereas Exodus supports over 100 different cryptocurrencies. Exodus will deduct network miner's fees for transactions but does not charge any extra transaction fees. Whether you decide to use a hardware wallet or a software wallet, start with small transfers such as $20 or less. After you gain confidence and experience with your cryptocurrency transfers, you can transfer larger amounts.

In summary:

- A cryptocurrency wallet is a method used to record and store information to access cryptocurrency.
- There are three types of wallets used to store this information. The three types are a paper wallet, a software wallet, and a hardware wallet.
- If you decide to purchase a hardware wallet, purchase it from the manufacturer not from a third-party vendor such as eBay or Amazon
- You can purchase the Ledger nano S at HTTPS: \\ www.ledger.com
- You can purchase the Trezor wallet at
- HTTPS:\\trezor. IO

Below are the Trezor and Ledger wallets, they have an USB port that you plug into your computer. (they look like flash drives)

Remember, only purchase your offline wallet directly from manufacturer, not Amazon or other alternate sites.

Chapter 8

Crypto Debit Cards

If you want to start using your cryptocurrency assets now for purchases, one option is to obtain a cryptocurrency debit card. Many merchants and private parties do not yet accept cryptocurrencies for the purchase of goods or services.

Today, several cryptocurrency exchanges will issue a debit card backed by Visa or MasterCard, these can be used just like any bank issued debit card to make purchases or withdraw cash from an ATM. There are at this time at least 10 different debit cards to choose from. You can choose to use a virtual debit card on your phone or order a physical card. I personally prefer the physical card I carry in my wallet.

Most crypto debit cards work by loading the card with a cryptocurrency supported by the exchange that issues the card. Then, when the card is used to make a purchase or withdraw cash from an ATM, the crypto currency will be converted into US dollar at the time of transaction.

Examples of these types of cards are the Visa card issued by Coinbase or MasterCard issued by Uphold. Another option is the MasterCard issued by BitPay, with this card cryptocurrency is converted into U.S. dollars at the time it is loaded onto the card. With the BitPay card the amount of the US dollar currency on the card stays the same and is not determined by the exchange rate at the time of purchase.

I use a BitPay card as I like to know the exact amount of the US dollar value on the card at the time of transaction. Investopedia.com does a good review on the different cards available, and the fees they charge, for example the Coinbase Visa card charge is a 2.5% transaction fee on purchases.

There are also withdrawal fees when using an ATM. The cryptocurrency market is volatile, and the dollar value may vary from day to day. This is a benefit if you use a card like the Coinbase Visa when the market is up. On the other hand, it could be a detriment if you use it when the exchange rate is down. There are also daily spending limits when using debit cards for withdrawals or purchases. There is a fee for ordering a physical debit card, usually between 10 to 12 dollars. Look at the comparisons on investopedia.com and do your own research if you decide to use a cryptocurrency debit card.

We were skeptical about whether the debit card would be accepted. We went ahead and ordered a card, from Bitpay, moved crypto onto it in the form of converted USD. Activated the card and went to the gas station. We were able to purchase gas with our new card, with no problems at all! The transaction went smoothly.

In summary:

- Today, several cryptocurrency exchanges will issue a debit card backed by Visa or MasterCard, these can be used just like any bank issued debit card to make purchases or withdraw cash from an ATM.
- Examples of these types of cards are the Visa card issued by Coinbase or MasterCard issued by Uphold. Another option is the MasterCard issued by BitPay, with this card cryptocurrency is converted into U.S. dollars at the time it is loaded onto the card.

Below is our Bitpay card with which we have made purchases at our local gas pump and grocer.

Chapter 9

Market Analysis

If you have decided after reading the previous chapters in this book that you are going to take the plunge and invest in the Cryptocurrency market, you may want to do some research before making your investment. Two of the most widely known methods used by cryptocurrency investors are called technical analysis and fundamental analysis.

Technical analysis looks at the historical performance of an asset, such as what was the all-time high value of an asset and when did it occur? Technical analysis would also include the high and low price of an asset over the past 24 hours, past week, and month. Other things to look at would be the volume of coins being bought or sold over the past 24 hours. Are more people buying or selling over the past 24 hours, and what is the total market cap? Market cap is the price of the asset multiplied by the total supply of coins or tokens in circulation. Technical analysis focuses on the price and volume of trading of an asset over a period of time.

In contrast, fundamental analysis looks at the overall information about an asset. This would include who the inventors and developers of the asset are. When was the asset first introduced? Who are the financial backers of the asset? Is the asset a cryptocurrency only, or is it a trading platform? Does the cryptocurrency have a real-world application and is it backed by a real-world corporation or business?

The goal of technical and fundamental analysis is to help you decide if an asset is undervalued or overvalued. This information can help you decide if and how much you want to invest in a cryptocurrency.

I suggest at a minimum you research how long the cryptocurrency has been available. Newly introduced assets carry more risks as well as possibly more potential for gain than more established cryptocurrencies such as Bitcoin, Ethereum or Litecoin for example. The best place I have found to find this information is at CoinGecko.com.

In closing, remember to never invest more than you can afford to lose. Slow and steady wins the race.

In summary:

- Technical analysis reviews and analyzes the historical value of an asset.
- Market cap is the price of the asset multiplied by the total supply of coins or tokens in circulation.
- Fundamental analysis reviews the information about the asset itself, such as who the inventors are, when it was first introduced and so on.
- . Newly introduced assets carry more risks as well as possibly more potential for gain than more established cryptocurrencies such as Bitcoin, Ethereum or Litecoin for example.
- The best place I have found to find this information is at CoinGecko.com.

Note below that Bitcoin was valued at 10 cents in 2010, today it is worth $46,000 and holding its own. There are many factors that play into the value of Bitcoin, such as market manipulation by whales (**Individuals or institutions who hold large amounts of coins of a certain cryptocurrency** are known as whales.)

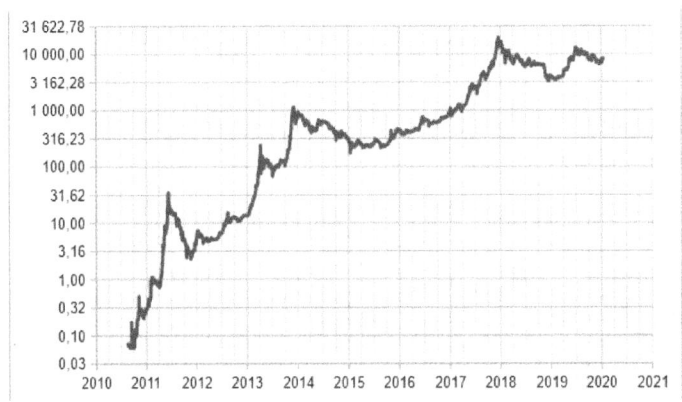

Chapter 10

Definitions

Below are a few terms you may encounter as you start you journey into the world of cryptocurrencies

Bagholder - Someone holding onto a coin that has plummeted in price.

Blockchain - A Bitcoin block contains information about the Sender, Receiver, number of bitcoins to be transferred.

Central bank – A national bank that operates to establish monetary and fiscal policy and to control the money supply and interest rate.

Cryptocurrency - A cryptocurrency is a type of currency which uses digital files as money. Usually, the files are created using the same ways as cryptography (the science of hiding information). Cryptocurrencies use 'decentralized control', which means that they aren't controlled by one person or government.

FOMO – Cryptocurrency slang for Fear of Missing Out

FUD – Cryptocurrency slang for Fear, Uncertainty and Doubt

KYC – Know your customer

Peer-to-peer bitcoin network - Peer-to-peer transactions are electronic money transfers made from one person to another through an intermediary, typically referred to as a P2P payment application.

HODL – A term derived from a misspelling of "hold" that refers to buy-and-hold strategies in the context of Bitcoin and other cryptocurrencies.

Market cap - Market cap is the price of the asset multiplied by the total supply of coins or tokens in circulation.

Pump and dump - Pump happens when a great ton of attention leads to a coin's price increase; dump happens when the coin's price crashes after an associated spread of negative emotions. It is used to manipulate markets.

Sats or Satoshi - The name given to the smallest unit of the Bitcoin cryptocurrency. It represents one hundred millionth of a Bitcoin.

Shill – Someone purposely promoting something for their own benefit.

Whale - An investor who owns five percent or more of any cryptocurrency coin.

Chapter 11

Blockchain Uses outside of Cryptocurrency

- **Healthcare setting**- A startup company, BlockMedx is utilizing blockchain technology provides continuity in patient care across various doctors and facilities.
- **Real estate companies** utilizing smart contracts
A smart contract is a self-executing contract with the terms of the agreement between buyer and seller being directly written into lines of code. The code and the agreements contained therein exist across a distributed, decentralized blockchain network. The code controls the execution, and transactions are trackable and irreversible.

- **NFTs- Non fungible tokens**-A non-fungible token is a unique digital asset. It can be a photo, a logo, a meme, a music album, a basketball highlight, a collage, a tweet, a newspaper article, a video; basically, anything that can get online. Blockchain can be used to prevent pirating copies or forging a unique digital form of art. The artist could receive royalties through each distributed copy of the art.
- There are many other uses and potential uses for blockchain technology, these are just a few for example

Sample Ledger

You can purchase this ledger on Amazon, it is a really handy tool. By the way I've seen some ledgers with a spot to put your password.

How to use this ledger

- Record what coin you are purchasing, and the date purchased.
- Record amount and price of coins purchased
- Keep track ever couple weeks to see how your coin is doing (increase/decrease/same.
- Decide if, at that point you are hodling (holding and not selling) or selling. Note with checkmark and add details in the notes section.
- If you purchase more coins then record as above, put a note in notes area.

STORE YOUR PASSWORDS SEPARATELY IN A SECURE LOCATION

BOOMERS LEDGER

COIN_____   DATE_____

DATE	$ EA COIN	# PURCHASED	HODL	SOLD	NOTES

Notes

ABOUT THE AUTHOR

Michael Lounsbury is a Baby Boomer, born in the middle of the Boomer era. He had spent his career as a physician assistant until 2020, when he found himself, like many in his profession out of a job due to the Covid-19 pandemic. During his time unemployed he furthered his knowledge and education in the field of cryptocurrency, starting with Bitcoin. As his knowledge and confidence grew, he realized there were thousands like him in the same boat-almost ready for retirement but watching their portfolios not performing as well as expected. He decided to reach out and educate his peers. The learning curve and understanding what cryptocurrencies are and what their use is in the ever-changing world can be intimidating. To that end, he wrote this book.

Join Mike on his You Tube channel: https://www.youtube.com/channel/ UCjB_8vU9i_y6b7blRZsHrivg

Email: cryptoforboomers@gmail.com

www.ingramcontent.com/pod-product-compliance
Lightning Source LLC
Chambersburg PA
CBHW030036230526
45472CB00002B/536